100 GREAT POEMS FOR GIRLS

Also edited by Celia Johnson

100 Poems to Lift Your Spirits

100 GREAT POEMS FOR GIRLS

CELIA JOHNSON

GC

GRAND CENTRAL
PUBLISHING

NEW YORK   BOSTON

Some poems have been reprinted by permission, which the editor and publisher gratefully acknowledge in detail in the Acknowledgments section of this book, beginning on page 183.

Grand Central Publishing
Hachette Book Group
237 Park Avenue
New York, NY 10017

www.HachetteBookGroup.com

Printed in the United States of America

First Edition: April 2011

10 9 8 7 6 5 4 3 2 1

Grand Central Publishing is a division of Hachette Book Group, Inc. The Grand Central Publishing name and logo is a trademark of Hachette Book Group, Inc.

The publisher is not responsible for websites (or their content) that are not owned by the publisher.

Library of Congress Cataloging-in-Publication Data

100 great poems for girls / [edited] by Celia Johnson.—1st ed.
    p. cm.
  Summary: "In the spirit of the Dangerous Book for Girls, here are 100 essential poems for girls of all ages"—Provided by publisher.
  ISBN 978-0-446-56384-0
  1. Girls—Poetry. 2. English poetry. 3. American poetry. 4. Children's poetry, English. 5. Children's poetry, American. I. Johnson, Celia.
II. Title: One hundred great poems for girls.
  PR1195.G5A16 2011
  821'.00803522—dc22
                   2010036491

Contents

Nature 1

Imagination 27

Inspiration 53

Animals   75

Nursery Rhymes   107

Limericks and Tongue Twisters   125

Fun and Nonsense 139

Introduction

The poems I remember most vividly as a little girl were the ones that we would chant as we sat in a circle and clapped our hands. But as I grew older, I discovered that a poem can be even more than rhymes sung together with friends. Poetry transports you to magical places, whether it's to the mythical Camelot in "The Lady of Shalott" or the edge of a bubbling cauldron in "Song of the Witches." The world around you transforms beneath the lens of poetry, bringing a field of golden daffodils to life and showing how a tiny spider spins its beautiful, intricate web. You'll find yourself laughing uncontrollably at the best humor and nonsense poems, where anything is possible, from an owl and a pussycat sailing out to sea to a courageous young girl gobbling up a nasty bear. And sometimes a poem acts like a best friend, making you feel like you're not alone.

There are no rules about how to experience poetry. Depending on your mood, you can read a poem on your own, tucked away in your room or lying in the grass on a summer day. Or you might read aloud with a friend, appreciating the rhythm and rhymes that a poet has carefully orchestrated in each stanza. It can be especially entertaining to read a limerick or tongue twister loud and fast, trying not to trip over tricky alliteration.

Whether you choose to memorize, read, or recite them aloud, each poem in this collection will offer something new—a spark of imagination, a unique rhyme, a vivid description, or simply a reason to laugh. These poems were surprising discoveries for me when I first encountered them, and they are even more special every time I read them again. I hope you feel the same way.

NATURE

Even in the biggest cities, there are signs of nature: a bright flower peeks out of a crack in the sidewalk, a vine climbs up the side of a building, spring rains wash over dusty streets. The natural world is present wherever we are, and each season brings a host of new growth with different colors, shapes, and smells. Nature can evoke powerful emotions, which might be why it inspires so many poets. Through the lens of poetry, a garden can bloom or a rose might simply be just a rose, and you'll see that the best way to learn about the stars is not in a classroom, but by looking up at the night sky.

A Girl's Garden

Robert Frost

A neighbor of mine in the village
    Likes to tell how one spring
When she was a girl on the farm, she did
    A childlike thing.

One day she asked her father
    To give her a garden plot
To plant and tend and reap herself,
    And he said, "Why not?"

In casting about for a corner
    He thought of an idle bit
Of walled-off ground where a shop had stood,
    And he said, "Just it."

And he said, "That ought to make you
    An ideal one-girl farm,
And give you a chance to put some strength
    On your slim-jim arm."

It was not enough of a garden,
    Her father said, to plough;
So she had to work it all by hand,
    But she don't mind now.

She wheeled the dung in the wheelbarrow
    Along a stretch of road;
But she always ran away and left
    Her not-nice load,

And hid from anyone passing.
    And then she begged the seed.
She says she thinks she planted one
    Of all things but weed.

A hill each of potatoes,
    Radishes, lettuce, peas,
Tomatoes, beets, beans, pumpkins, corn,
    And even fruit trees.

And yes, she has long mistrusted
    That a cider apple tree
In bearing there to-day is hers,
    Or at least may be.

Her crop was a miscellany
    When all was said and done,
A little bit of everything,
    A great deal of none.

Now when she sees in the village
    How village things go,
Just when it seems to come in right,
    She says, "*I* know!

It's as when I was a farmer—"
    Oh, never by way of advice!
And she never sins by telling the tale
    To the same person twice.

The Rose Family

Robert Frost

The rose is a rose,
And was always a rose.
But the theory now goes
That the apple's a rose,
And the pear is, and so's
The peach, I suppose.
The dear only knows
What will next prove a rose.
You of course are a rose—
But were always a rose.

The Daffodils

William Wordsworth

I wandered lonely as a cloud
That floats on high o'er vales and hills,
When all at once I saw a crowd,
A host, of golden daffodils;
Beside the lake, beneath the trees,
Fluttering and dancing in the breeze.

Continuous as the stars that shine
And twinkle on the milky way,
They stretched in never-ending line
Along the margin of a bay:
Ten thousand saw I at a glance,
Tossing their heads in sprightly dance.

The waves beside them danced; but they
Out-did the sparkling waves in glee:
A poet could not but be gay,
In such a jocund company:
I gazed—and gazed—but little thought
What wealth the show to me had brought:

For oft, when on my couch I lie
In vacant or in pensive mood,
They flash upon that inward eye
Which is the bliss of solitude;
And then my heart with pleasure fills,
And dances with the daffodils.

To the Daisy

William Wordsworth

In youth from rock to rock I went,
From hill to hill in discontent
Of pleasure high and turbulent,
    Most pleased when most uneasy;
But now my own delights I make,—
My thirst at every rill can slake,
And gladly Nature's love partake,
    Of Thee, sweet Daisy!

Thee Winter in the garland wears
That thinly decks his few gray hairs;
Spring parts the clouds with softest airs,
    That she may sun thee;
Whole Summer-fields are thine by right;
And Autumn, melancholy Wight!
Doth in thy crimson head delight
    When rains are on thee.

In shoals and bands, a morrice train,
Thou greet'st the traveler in the lane;
Pleased at his greeting thee again;
    Yet nothing daunted,

Nor grieved if thou be set at nought:
And oft alone in nooks remote
We meet thee, like a pleasant thought,
    When such are wanted.

Be violets in their secret mews
The flowers the wanton Zephyrs choose;
Proud be the rose, with rains and dews
    Her head impearling,
Thou liv'st with less ambitious aim,
Yet hast not gone without thy fame;
Thou art indeed by many a claim
    The Poet's darling.

If to a rock from rains he fly,
Or, some bright day of April sky,
Imprisoned by hot sunshine lie
    Near the green holly,
And wearily at length should fare;
He needs but look about; and there
Thou art!—a friend at hand, to scare
    His melancholy.

A hundred times, by rock or bower,
Ere thus I have lain couched an hour,
Have I derived from thy sweet power
    Some apprehension;

Some steady love; some brief delight;
Some memory that had taken flight;
Some chime of fancy wrong or right;
  Or stray invention.

If stately passions in me burn,
And one chance look to Thee should turn,
I drink out of an humbler urn
  A lowlier pleasure;
The homely sympathy that heeds
The common life, our nature breeds;
A wisdom fitted to the needs
  Of hearts at leisure.

Fresh-smitten by the morning ray,
When thou art up, alert and gay,
Then, cheerful Flower! my spirits play
  With kindred gladness:
And when, at dusk, by dews opprest
Thou sink'st, the image of thy rest
Hath often eased my pensive breast
  Of careful sadness.

And all day long I number yet,
All seasons through, another debt,
Which I, wherever thou art met,
  To thee am owing;

An instinct call it, a blind sense;
A happy, genial influence,
Coming one knows not how, nor whence,
      Nor whither going.

Child of the Year! that round dost run
Thy pleasant course,—when day's begun
As ready to salute the sun
      As lark or leveret,
Thy long-lost praise thou shalt regain;
Nor be less dear to future men
Than in old time;—thou not in vain
      Art Nature's favorite.

The Rhodora

ON BEING ASKED, WHENCE IS THE FLOWER?

Ralph Waldo Emerson

In May, when sea-winds pierced our solitudes,
I found the fresh Rhodora in the woods,
Spreading its leafless blooms in a damp nook,
To please the desert and the sluggish brook.
The purple petals, fallen in the pool,
Made the black water with their beauty gay;
Here might the red-bird come his plumes to cool,
And court the flower that cheapens his array.
Rhodora! if the sages ask thee why
This charm is wasted on the earth and sky,
Tell them, dear, that if eyes were made for seeing,
Then Beauty is its own excuse for being:
Why thou wert there, O rival of the rose!
I never thought to ask, I never knew:
But, in my simple ignorance, suppose
The self-same Power that brought me there brought you.

Counting-Out Rhyme

Edna St. Vincent Millay

Silver bark of beech, and sallow
Bark of yellow birch and yellow
   Twig of willow.

Stripe of green in moosewood maple,
Color seen in leaf of apple,
   Bark of popple.

Wood of popple pale as moonbeam,
Wood of oak for yoke and barn-beam
   Wood of hornbeam.

Silver bark of beech, and hollow
Stem of elder, tall and yellow
   Twig of willow.

To the First Robin

Louisa May Alcott

Welcome, welcome, little stranger,
Fear no harm, and fear no danger;
We are glad to see you here,
For you sing "Sweet Spring is near."

Now the white snow melts away;
Now the flowers blossom gay:
Come dear bird and build your nest,
For we love our robin best.

Spring

Gerard Manley Hopkins

Nothing is so beautiful as spring—
   When weeds, in wheels, shoot long and lovely and lush;
   Thrush's eggs look little low heavens, and thrush
Through the echoing timber does so rinse and wring
The ear, it strikes like lightnings to hear him sing;
   The glassy peartree leaves and blooms, they brush
   The descending blue; that blue is all in a rush
With richness; the racing lambs too have fair their fling.

What is all this juice and all this joy?
   A strain of the earth's sweet being in the beginning
In Eden garden.—Have, get, before it cloy,
   Before it cloud, Christ, lord, and sour with sinning,
Innocent mind and Mayday in girl and boy,
   Most, O maid's child, thy choice and worthy the winning.

April Rain Song

Langston Hughes

Let the rain kiss you.
Let the rain beat upon your head with silver liquid drops.
Let the rain sing you a lullaby.

The rain makes still pools on the sidewalk.
The rain makes running pools in the gutter.
The rain plays a little sleep-song on our roof at night—

And I love the rain.

Fog

Carl Sandburg

The fog comes
on little cat feet.

It sits looking
over harbor and city
on silent haunches
and then moves on.

The Cloud

Percy Bysshe Shelley

I bring fresh showers for the thirsting flowers,
    From the seas and the streams;
I bear light shade for the leaves when laid
    In their noonday dreams.
From my wings are shaken the dews that waken
    The sweet buds every one,
When rocked to rest on their mother's breast,
    As she dances about the sun.
I wield the flail of the lashing hail,
    And whiten the green plains under,
And then again I dissolve it in rain,
    And laugh as I pass in thunder.

I sift the snow on the mountains below,
    And their great pines groan aghast;
And all the night 'tis my pillow white,
    While I sleep in the arms of the blast.
Sublime on the towers of my skyey bowers,
    Lightning my pilot sits;
In a cavern under is fettered the thunder,
    It struggles and howls at fits;
Over earth and ocean, with gentle motion,
    This pilot is guiding me,
Lured by the love of the genii that move
    In the depths of the purple sea;

Over the rills, and the crags, and the hills,
    Over the lakes and the plains,
Wherever he dream, under mountain or stream,
    The Spirit he loves remains;
And I all the while bask in Heaven's blue smile,
    Whilst he is dissolving in rains.

The sanguine Sunrise, with his meteor eyes,
    And his burning plumes outspread,
Leaps on the back of my sailing rack,
    When the morning star shines dead;
As on the jag of a mountain crag,
    Which an earthquake rocks and swings,
An eagle alit one moment may sit
    In the light of its golden wings.
And when Sunset may breathe, from the lit sea beneath,
    Its ardors of rest and of love,
And the crimson pall of eve may fall
    From the depth of Heaven above,
With wings folded I rest, on mine airy nest,
    As still as a brooding dove.

That orbèd maiden with white fire laden,
    Whom mortals call the Moon,
Glides glimmering o'er my fleecelike floor,
    By the midnight breezes strewn;
And wherever the beat of her unseen feet,
    Which only the angels hear,
May have broken the woof of my tent's thin roof,
    The stars peep behind her and peer;

And I laugh to see them whirl and flee,
    Like a swarm of golden bees,
When I widen the rent in my wind-built tent,
    Till the calm rivers, lakes, and seas,
Like strips of the sky fallen through me on high,
    Are each paved with the moon and these.

I bind the Sun's throne with a burning zone,
    And the Moon's with a girdle of pearl;
The volcanoes are dim, and the stars reel and swim,
    When the whirlwinds my banner unfurl.
From cape to cape, with a bridgelike shape,
    Over a torrent sea,
Sunbeam-proof, I hang like a roof—
    The mountains its columns be.
The triumphal arch through which I march
    With hurricane, fire, and snow,
When the Powers of the air are chained to my chair,
    Is the million-colored bow;
The sphere-fire above its soft colors wove,
    While the moist Earth was laughing below.

I am the daughter of Earth and Water,
    And the nursling of the Sky;
I pass through the pores of the ocean and shores;
    I change, but I cannot die.
For after the rain when with never a stain
    The pavilion of Heaven is bare,
And the winds and sunbeams with their convex gleams
    Build up the blue dome of air,

I silently laugh at my own cenotaph,
    And out of the caverns of rain,
Like a child from the womb, like a ghost from the tomb,
    I arise and unbuild it again.

Who Has Seen the Wind?

Christina Rossetti

Who has seen the wind?
  Neither I nor you:
But when the leaves hang trembling
  The wind is passing thro'.

Who has seen the wind?
  Neither you nor I:
But when the trees bow down their heads
  The wind is passing by.

What Is Pink?

Christina Rossetti

What is pink? a rose is pink
By the fountain's brink.
What is red? a poppy's red
In its barley bed.
What is blue? the sky is blue
Where the clouds float thro'.
What is white? a swan is white
Sailing in the light.
What is yellow? pears are yellow,
Rich and ripe and mellow.
What is green? the grass is green,
With small flowers between.
What is violet? clouds are violet
In the summer twilight.
What is orange? why, an orange,
Just an orange!

When I Heard the Learn'd Astronomer

Walt Whitman

When I heard the learn'd astronomer,
When the proofs, the figures, were ranged in columns
    before me,
When I was shown the charts and diagrams, to add, divide,
    and measure them,
When I sitting heard the astronomer where he lectured
    with much applause in the lecture-room,
How soon unaccountable I became tired and sick,
Till rising and gliding out I wander'd off by myself,
In the mystical moist night-air, and from time to time,
Look'd up in perfect silence at the stars.

The Grass So Little Has to Do

Emily Dickinson

The Grass so little has to do —
A Sphere of simple Green —
With only Butterflies to brood
And Bees to entertain —

And stir all day to pretty Tunes
The Breezes fetch along —
And hold the Sunshine in its lap
And bow to everything —

And thread the Dews, all night, like Pearls —
And make itself so fine
A Duchess were too common
For such a noticing —

And even when it dies — to pass
In Odors so divine —
Like Lowly spices, lain to sleep —
Or Spikenards, perishing —

And then, in Sovereign Barns to dwell —
And dream the Days away,
The Grass so little has to do
I wish I were a Hay —

IMAGINATION

A poem can carry you away to another world, just like your most vivid dreams. Samuel Taylor Coleridge wrote "Kubla Khan" after waking up from a dream that lingered in his mind, and he rebuilt that vision with each line and stanza. There are no boundaries to the enchanting places and characters that come to life in a poem, whether it is a charming fairy or a bold little orphan girl. And while reading Shakespeare's "Song of the Witches," you may even find that you've transformed into a cackling witch. In "To Imagination," Emily Brontë understands precisely how powerful an imagination can be, offering an escape, even if it's brief, from the world around you. Each of these poems is designed to do just that.

To Imagination

Emily Brontë

When weary with the long day's care,
   And earthly change from pain to pain,
And lost and ready to despair,
   Thy kind voice calls me back again:
Oh, my true friend! I am not lone,
While thou canst speak with such a tone!

So hopeless is the world without;
   The world within I doubly prize;
Thy world, where guile, and hate, and doubt,
   And cold suspicion never rise;
Where thou, and I, and Liberty,
Have undisputed sovereignty.

What matters it, that, all around,
   Danger, and guilt, and darkness lie,
If but within our bosom's bound
   We hold a bright, untroubled sky.
Warm with ten thousand mingled rays
Of suns that know no winter days?

Reason, indeed, may oft complain
    For Nature's sad reality,
And tell the suffering heart, how vain
    Its cherished dreams must always be;
And Truth may rudely trample down
The flowers of Fancy, newly-blown:

But, thou art ever there, to bring
    The hovering vision back, and breathe
New glories o'er the blighted spring,
    And call a lovelier Life from Death,
And whisper, with a voice divine,
Of real worlds, as bright as thine.

I trust not to thy phantom bliss,
    Yet, still, in evening's quiet hour,
With never-failing thankfulness,
    I welcome thee, Benignant Power;
Sure solacer of human cares,
And sweeter hope, when hope despairs!

The Lady of Shalott

Alfred, Lord Tennyson

Part 1

On either side the river lie
Long fields of barley and of rye,
That clothe the wold and meet the sky;
And through the field the road runs by
       To many towered Camelot;
And up and down the people go,
Gazing where the lilies blow
Round an island there below,
       The island of Shalott.

Willows whiten, aspens quiver,
Little breezes dusk and shiver
Through the wave that runs for ever
By the island in the river
       Flowing down to Camelot.
Four gray walls, and four gray towers,
Overlook a space of flowers,
And the silent isle imbowers
       The Lady of Shalott.

By the margin, willow-veiled,
Slide the heavy barges trailed
By slow horses; and unhailed
The shallop flitteth silken-sailed
      Skimming down to Camelot:
But who hath seen her wave her hand?
Or at the casement seen her stand?
Or is she known in all the land,
      The Lady of Shalott?

Only reapers, reaping early
In among the bearded barley,
Hear a song that echoes cheerly
From the river winding clearly,
      Down to towered Camelot:
And by the moon the reaper weary,
Piling sheaves in uplands airy,
Listening, whispers " 'Tis the fairy
      Lady of Shalott."

Part 2
There she weaves by night and day
A magic web with colors gay.
She has heard a whisper say,
A curse is on her if she stay
      To look down to Camelot.

She knows not what the curse may be,
And so she weaveth steadily,
And little other care hath she,
        The Lady of Shalott.

And moving through a mirror clear
That hangs before her all the year,
Shadows of the world appear.
There she sees the highway near
        Winding down to Camelot:
There the river eddy whirls,
And there the surly village-churls,
And the red cloaks of market girls,
        Pass onward from Shalott.

Sometimes a troop of damsels glad,
An abbot on an ambling pad,
Sometimes a curly shepherd-lad,
Or long-haired page in crimson clad,
        Goes by to towered Camelot;
And sometimes through the mirror blue
The knights come riding two and two:
She hath no loyal knight and true,
        The Lady of Shalott.

But in her web she still delights
To weave the mirror's magic sights,
For often through the silent nights
A funeral, with plumes and lights
        And music, went to Camelot:

Or when the moon was overhead,
Came two young lovers lately wed;
"I am half sick of shadows," said
  The Lady of Shalott.

   Part 3
A bow-shot from her bower-eaves,
He rode between the barley-sheaves,
The sun came dazzling through the leaves,
And flamed upon the brazen greaves
  Of bold Sir Lancelot.
A red-cross knight for ever kneeled
To a lady in his shield,
That sparkled on the yellow field,
  Beside remote Shalott.

The gemmy bridle glittered free,
Like to some branch of stars we see
Hung in the golden Galaxy.
The bridle bells rang merrily
  As he rode down to Camelot:
And from his blazoned baldric slung
A mighty silver bugle hung,
And as he rode his armor rung,
  Beside remote Shalott.

All in the blue unclouded weather
Thick-jeweled shone the saddle-leather,
The helmet and the helmet-feather
Burned like one burning flame together,
    As he rode down to Camelot.
As often through the purple night,
Below the starry clusters bright,
Some bearded meteor, trailing light,
    Moves over still Shalott.

His broad clear brow in sunlight glowed;
On burnished hooves his war-horse trode;
From underneath his helmet flowed
His coal-black curls as on he rode,
    As he rode down to Camelot.
From the bank and from the river
He flashed into the crystal mirror,
"Tirra lirra," by the river
    Sang Sir Lancelot.

She left the web, she left the loom,
She made three paces through the room,
She saw the water-lily bloom,
She saw the helmet and the plume,
    She looked down to Camelot.
Out flew the web and floated wide;
The mirror cracked from side to side;
"The curse is come upon me," cried
    The Lady of Shalott.

Part 4

In the stormy east-wind straining,
The pale yellow woods were waning,
The broad stream in his banks complaining.
Heavily the low sky raining
    Over towered Camelot;
Down she came and found a boat
Beneath a willow left afloat,
And round about the prow she wrote
    The Lady of Shalott.

And down the river's dim expanse
Like some bold seer in a trance,
Seeing all his own mischance—
With a glassy countenance
    Did she look to Camelot.
And at the closing of the day
She loosed the chain, and down she lay;
The broad stream bore her far away,
    The Lady of Shalott.

Lying, robed in snowy white
That loosely flew to left and right—
The leaves upon her falling light—
Through the noises of the night
    She floated down to Camelot:
And as the boat-head wound along
The willowy hills and fields among,
They heard her singing her last song,
    The Lady of Shalott.

Heard a carol, mournful, holy,
Chanted loudly, chanted lowly,
Till her blood was frozen slowly,
And her eyes were darkened wholly,
    Turned to towered Camelot.
For ere she reached upon the tide
The first house by the water-side,
Singing in her song she died,
    The Lady of Shalott.

Under tower and balcony,
By garden-wall and gallery,
A gleaming shape she floated by,
Dead-pale between the houses high,
    Silent into Camelot.
Out upon the wharfs they came,
Knight and burgher, lord and dame,
And round the prow they read her name,
    The Lady of Shalott.

Who is this? and what is here?
And in the lighted palace near
Died the sound of royal cheer;
And they crossed themselves for fear,
    All the knights at Camelot:
But Lancelot mused a little space;
He said, "She has a lovely face;
God in his mercy lend her grace,
    The Lady of Shalott."

Song of the Witches

William Shakespeare

Double, double, toil and trouble,
Fire burn and cauldron bubble.
Fillet of a fenny snake,
In the cauldron boil and bake;
Eye of newt, and toe of frog,
Wool of bat, and tongue of dog,
Adder's fork, and blind worm's sting,
Lizard's leg, and howlet's wing—
For a charm of pow'rful trouble
Like a hell-broth boil and bubble.
Double, double, toil and trouble,
Fire burn and cauldron bubble.
Scale of dragon, tooth of wolf,
Witch's mummy, maw and gulf
Of the ravined salt-sea shark,
Root of hemlock digged i' th' dark,
Liver of blaspheming Jew,
Gall of goat, and slips of yew
Slivered in the moon's eclipse,
Nose of Turk, and Tartar's lips,
Finger of birth-strangled babe
Ditch-delivered by a drab
Make the gruel thick and slab.
Add thereto a tiger's chaudron
For th' ingredient of our cauldron.

Double, double, toil and trouble,
Fire burn and cauldron bubble.
Cool it with a baboon's blood,
Then the charm is firm and good.

La Belle Dame sans Merci

A BALLAD

John Keats

O what can ail thee, knight-at-arms,
    Alone and palely loitering?
The sedge has withered from the lake,
    And no birds sing.

O what can ail thee, knight-at-arms,
    So haggard and so woe-begone?
The squirrel's granary is full,
    And the harvest's done.

I see a lily on thy brow,
    With anguish moist and fever-dew,
And on thy cheeks a fading rose
    Fast withereth too.

I met a lady in the meads,
    Full beautiful—a faery's child,
Her hair was long, her foot was light,
    And her eyes were wild.

I made a garland for her head,
    And bracelets too, and fragrant zone;
She looked at me as she did love,
    And made sweet moan.

I set her on my pacing steed,
   And nothing else saw all day long,
For sidelong would she bend, and sing
   A faery's song.

She found me roots of relish sweet,
   And honey wild, and manna-dew,
And sure in language strange she said—
   "I love thee true."

She took me to her elfin grot,
   And there she wept and sighed full sore,
And there I shut her wild wild eyes
   With kisses four.

And there she lullèd me asleep
   And there I dreamed—Ah! woe betide!—
The latest dream I ever dreamt
   On the cold hill side.

I saw pale kings and princes too,
   Pale warriors, death-pale were they all;
They cried—"La Belle Dame sans Merci
   Thee hath in thrall!"

I saw their starved lips in the gloam,
   With horrid warning gapèd wide,
And I awoke and found me here,
   On the cold hill's side.

And this is why I sojourn here
   Alone and palely loitering,
Though the sedge is withered from the lake,
   And no birds sing.

Kubla Khan

OR A VISION IN A DREAM. A FRAGMENT

Samuel Taylor Coleridge

In Xanadu did Kubla Khan
A stately pleasure dome decree:
Where Alph, the sacred river, ran
Through caverns measureless to man
    Down to a sunless sea.
So twice five miles of fertile ground
With walls and towers were girdled round:
And there were gardens bright with sinuous rills,
Where blossomed many an incense-bearing tree;
And here were forests ancient as the hills,
Enfolding sunny spots of greenery.

But oh! that deep romantic chasm which slanted
Down the green hill athwart a cedarn cover!
A savage place! as holy and enchanted
As e'er beneath a waning moon was haunted
By woman wailing for her demon lover!
And from this chasm, with ceaseless turmoil seething,
As if this earth in fast thick pants were breathing,
A mighty fountain momently was forced:
Amid whose swift half-intermitted burst
Huge fragments vaulted like rebounding hail,
Or chaffy grain beneath the thresher's flail:
And 'mid these dancing rocks at once and ever

It flung up momently the sacred river.
Five miles meandering with a mazy motion
Through wood and dale the sacred river ran,
Then reached the caverns measureless to man,
And sank in tumult to a lifeless ocean:
And 'mid this tumult Kubla heard from far
Ancestral voices prophesying war!

    The shadow of the dome of pleasure
    Floated midway on the waves;
    Where was heard the mingled measure
    From the fountain and the caves.
It was a miracle of rare device,
A sunny pleasure dome with caves of ice!

    A damsel with a dulcimer
    In a vision once I saw:
    It was an Abyssinian maid,
    And on her dulcimer she played,
    Singing of Mount Abora.
    Could I revive within me
    Her symphony and song,
    To such a deep delight 'twould win me,
That with music loud and long,
I would build that dome in air,
That sunny dome! those caves of ice!
And all who heard should see them there,
And all should cry, Beware! Beware!

His flashing eyes, his floating hair!
Weave a circle round him thrice,
And close your eyes with holy dread,
For he on honey-dew hath fed,
And drunk the milk of Paradise.

The Song of Wandering Aengus

William Butler Yeats

I went out to the hazel wood,
Because a fire was in my head,
And cut and peeled a hazel wand,
And hooked a berry to a thread;
And when white moths were on the wing,
And moth-like stars were flickering out,
I dropped the berry in a stream
And caught a little silver trout.

When I had laid it on the floor
I went to blow the fire a-flame,
But something rustled on the floor,
And someone called me by my name:
It had become a glimmering girl
With apple blossom in her hair
Who called me by my name and ran
And faded through the brightening air.

Though I am old with wandering
Through hollow lands and hilly lands,
I will find out where she has gone,
And kiss her lips and take her hands;
And walk among long dappled grass,
And pluck till time and times are done,
The silver apples of the moon,
The golden apples of the sun.

Little Orphant Annie

James Whitcomb Riley

Little Orphant Annie's come to our house to stay,
An' wash the cups an' saucers up, an' brush the crumbs away,
An' shoo the chickens off the porch, an' dust the hearth, an'
    sweep,
An' make the fire, an' bake the bread, an' earn her board-
    an'-keep;
An' all us other children, when the supper things is done,
We set around the kitchen fire an' has the mostest fun
A-list'nin' to the witch-tales 'at Annie tells about,
An' the Gobble-uns 'at gits you
      Ef you
        Don't
          Watch
            Out!

Onc't they was a little boy wouldn't say his prayers,—
An' when he went to bed at night, away up stairs,
His Mammy heered him holler, an' his Daddy heered him
    bawl,
An' when they turn't the kivvers down, he wasn't there at all!
An' they seeked him in the rafter-room, an' cubby-hole, an'
    press,
An' seeked him up the chimbly-flue, an' ever'wheres, I guess;

But all they ever found was thist his pants an'
   roundabout:—
An' the Gobble-uns'll git you
     Ef you
       Don't
         Watch
           Out!

An' one time a little girl 'ud allus laugh an' grin,
An' make fun of ever'one, an' all her blood an' kin;
An' onc't, when they was "company," an' ole folks was
   there,
She mocked 'em an' shocked 'em, an' said she didn't care!
An' thist as she kicked her heels, an' turn't to run an' hide,
They was two great big Black Things a-standin' by her side,
An' they snatched her through the ceilin' 'fore she knowed
   what she's about!
An' the Gobble-uns'll git you
     Ef you
       Don't
         Watch
           Out!

An' little Orphant Annie says, when the blaze is blue,
An' the lamp-wick sputters, an' the wind goes *woo-oo!*
An' you hear the crickets quit, an' the moon is gray,
An' the lightnin'-bugs in dew is all squenched away,—
You better mind yer parents, an' yer teachers fond an' dear,

An' churish them 'at loves you, an' dry the orphant's tear,
An' he'p the pore an' needy ones 'at clusters all about,
Er the Gobble-uns'll git you
              Ef you
                Don't
                  Watch
                    Out!

The Opening of the Piano

Oliver Wendell Holmes

In the little southern parlor of the house you may have
    seen
With the gambrel-roof, and the gable looking westward to
    the green,
At the side toward the sunset, with the window on its right,
Stood the London-made piano I am dreaming of to-night.

Ah me! how I remember the evening when it came!
What a cry of eager voices, what a group of cheeks in
    flame,
When the wondrous box was opened that had come from
    over seas,
With its smell of mastic-varnish and its flash of ivory keys!

Then the children all grew fretful in the restlessness of joy,
For the boy would push his sister, and the sister crowd
    the boy,
Till the father asked for quiet in his grave paternal way,
But the mother hushed the tumult with the words, "Now,
    Mary, play."

For the dear soul knew that music was a very sovereign
  balm;
She had sprinkled it over Sorrow and seen its brow grow
  calm,
In the days of slender harpsichords with tapping tinkling
  quills,
Or carolling to her spinet with its thin metallic thrills.

So Mary, the household minstrel, who always loved to
  please,
Sat down to the new "Clementi," and struck the glittering
  keys.
Hushed were the children's voices, and every eye grew dim,
As, floating from lip and finger, arose the "Vesper Hymn."

—Catharine, child of a neighbor, curly and rosy-red,
(Wedded since, and a widow,—something like ten years
  dead,)
Hearing a gush of music such as none before,
Steals from her mother's chamber and peeps at the open
  door.

Just as the "Jubilate" in threaded whisper dies,
—"Open it! open it, lady!" the little maiden cries,
(For she thought 'twas a singing creature caged in a box she
  heard,)
"Open it! open it, lady! and let me see the *bird*!"

Where the Sidewalk Ends

Shel Silverstein

There is a place where the sidewalk ends
And before the street begins,
And there the grass grows soft and white,
And there the sun burns crimson bright,
And there the moon-bird rests from his flight
To cool in the peppermint wind.

Let us leave this place where the smoke blows black
And the dark street winds and bends.
Past the pits where the asphalt flowers grow
We shall walk with a walk that is measured and slow,
And watch where the chalk-white arrows go
To the place where the sidewalk ends.

Yes we'll walk with a walk that is measured and slow,
And we'll go where the chalk-white arrows go,
For the children, they mark, and the children, they know
The place where the sidewalk ends.

INSPIRATION

A spark of inspiration can illuminate the world around you in ways you might never have considered. Suddenly an overgrown path is full of possibility, an ancient urn holds secrets from the past, and being nobody isn't so bad after all. To be inspired is to leap toward a new thought or feeling as though you are taking flight. Emily Dickinson captures it perfectly when she describes hope as a thing with feathers.

"Hope" Is the Thing with Feathers

Emily Dickinson

"Hope" is the thing with feathers —
That perches in the soul —
And sings the tune without the words —
And never stops — at all —

And sweetest — in the Gale — is heard —
And sore must be the storm —
That could abash the little Bird
That kept so many warm —

I've heard it in the chillest land —
And on the strangest Sea —
Yet — never — in Extremity,
It asked a crumb — of me.

The Road Not Taken

Robert Frost

Two roads diverged in a yellow wood,
And sorry I could not travel both
And be one traveler, long I stood
And looked down one as far as I could
To where it bent in the undergrowth;

Then took the other, as just as fair,
And having perhaps the better claim,
Because it was grassy and wanted wear;
Though as for that the passing there
Had worn them really about the same,

And both that morning equally lay
In leaves no step had trodden black.
Oh, I kept the first for another day!
Yet knowing how way leads on to way,
I doubted if I should ever come back.

I shall be telling this with a sigh
Somewhere ages and ages hence:
Two roads diverged in a wood, and I—
I took the one less traveled by,
And that has made all the difference.

An Emerald Is as Green as Grass

Christina Rossetti

An emerald is as green as grass;
   A ruby red as blood;
A sapphire shines as blue as heaven;
   A flint lies in the mud.

A diamond is a brilliant stone,
   To catch the world's desire;
An opal holds a fiery spark;
   But a flint holds fire.

The Prologue

Anne Bradstreet

1

To sing of Wars, of Captaines, and of Kings,
Of Cities founded, Common-wealths begun,
For my mean Pen, are too superiour things,
And how they all, or each, their dates have run:
Let Poets, and Historians set these forth,
My obscure Verse, shal not so dim their worth.

2

But when my wondring eyes, and envious heart,
Great *Bartas* sugar'd lines doe but read o're;
Foole, *I* doe grudge, the Muses did not part
'Twixt him and me, that over-fluent store;
A *Bartas* can, doe what a *Bartas* wil,
But simple I, according to my skill.

3

From School-boyes tongue, no Rhethorick we expect,
Nor yet a sweet Confort, from broken strings,
Nor perfect beauty, where's a maine defect,
My foolish, broken, blemish'd Muse so sings;
And this to mend, alas, no Art is able,
'Cause Nature made it so irreparable.

4

Nor can I, like that fluent sweet tongu'd *Greek*
Who lisp'd at first, speake afterwards more plaine
By Art, he gladly found what he did seeke,
A full requitall of his striving paine:
Art can doe much, but this maxime's most sure,
A weake or wounded braine admits no cure.

5

I am obnoxious to each carping tongue,
Who sayes, my hand a needle better fits,
A Poets Pen, all scome, I should thus wrong;
For such despight they cast on female wits:
If what I doe prove well, it wo'nt advance,
They'l say its stolne, or else, it was by chance.

6

But sure the antick *Greeks* were far more milde,
Else of our Sex, why feigned they those nine,
And poesy made, *Calliope's* owne childe,
So 'mongst the rest, they plac'd the Arts divine:
But this weake knot they will full soone untye,
The *Greeks* did nought, but play the foole and lye.

7

Let *Greeks* be *Greeks*, and Women what they are,
Men have precedency, and still excell,
It is but vaine, unjustly to wage war,
Men can doe best, and Women know it well;
Preheminence in each, and all is yours,
Yet grant some small acknowledgement of ours.

8

And oh, ye high flown quils, that soare the skies,
And ever with your prey, still catch your praise,
If e're you daigne these lowly lines, your eyes
Give wholsome Parsley wreath, I aske no Bayes:
This meane and unrefined stuffe of mine,
Will make your glistering gold but more to shine.

Ode on a Grecian Urn

John Keats

Thou still unravished bride of quietness,
  Thou foster-child of silence and slow time,
Sylvan historian, who canst thus express
  A flowery tale more sweetly than our rhyme:
What leaf-fringed legend haunts about thy shape
  Of deities or mortals, or of both,
    In Tempe or the dales of Arcady?
  What men or gods are these? What maidens loth?
What mad pursuit? What struggle to escape?
    What pipes and timbrels? What wild ecstasy?

Heard melodies are sweet, but those unheard
  Are sweeter; therefore, ye soft pipes, play on;
Not to the sensual ear, but, more endeared,
  Pipe to the spirit ditties of no tone:
Fair youth, beneath the trees, thou canst not leave
  Thy song, nor ever can those trees be bare;
    Bold Lover, never, never canst thou kiss,
Though winning near the goal—yet, do not grieve:
    She cannot fade, though thou hast not thy bliss,
  For ever wilt thou love, and she be fair!

Ah, happy, happy boughs! that cannot shed
  Your leaves, nor ever bid the Spring adieu;

And, happy melodist, unwearièd,
   For ever piping songs for ever new;
More happy love! more happy, happy love!
   For ever warm and still to be enjoyed,
      For ever panting, and for ever young—
All breathing human passion far above,
   That leaves a heart high-sorrowful and cloyed,
      A burning forehead, and a parching tongue.

Who are these coming to the sacrifice?
   To what green altar, O mysterious priest,
Lead'st thou that heifer lowing at the skies,
   And all her silken flanks with garlands dressed?
What little town by river or sea shore,
   Or mountain-built with peaceful citadel,
      Is emptied of this folk, this pious morn?
And, little town, thy streets for evermore
   Will silent be; and not a soul to tell
      Why thou art desolate, can e'er return.

O Attic shape! Fair attitude! with brede
   Of marble men and maidens overwrought,
With forest branches and the trodden weed;
   Thou, silent form, dost tease us out of thought
As doth eternity: Cold Pastoral!
   When old age shall this generation waste,
      Thou shalt remain, in midst of other woe
   Than ours, a friend to man, to whom thou say'st,
"Beauty is truth, truth beauty,—that is all
      Ye know on earth, and all ye need to know."

The Lamb

William Blake

Little Lamb, who made thee?
  Dost thou know who made thee?
Gave thee life & bid thee feed,
By the stream & o'er the mead;
Gave thee clothing of delight,
Softest clothing wooly bright;
Gave thee such a tender voice,
Making all the vales rejoice!
  Little Lamb who made thee?
  Dost thou know who made thee?

Little Lamb I'll tell thee,
  Little Lamb I'll tell thee!
He is calléd by thy name,
For he calls himself a Lamb:
He is meek & he is mild,
He became a little child:
I a child & thou a lamb,
We are calléd by his name.
  Little Lamb God bless thee.
  Little Lamb God bless thee.

Sonnet 18

William Shakespeare

Shall I compare thee to a summer's day?
Thou art more lovely and more temperate.
Rough winds do shake the darling buds of May,
And summer's lease hath all too short a date.
Sometime too hot the eye of heaven shines,
And often is his gold complexion dimmed;
And every fair from fair sometime declines,
By chance, or nature's changing course, untrimmed:
But thy eternal summer shall not fade
Nor lose possession of that fair thou ow'st,
Nor shall Death brag thou wand'rest in his shade
When in eternal lines to time thou grow'st.
   So long as men can breathe or eyes can see,
   So long lives this, and this gives life to thee.

A Few Rules for Beginners

Katherine Mansfield

Babies must not eat the coal
And they must not make grimaces,
Nor in party dresses roll
And must never black their faces.

They must learn that pointing's rude,
They must sit quite still at table,
And must always eat the food
Put before them—if they're able.

If they fall, they must not cry,
Though it's known how painful this is;
No—there's always Mother by
Who will comfort them with kisses.

A Little Girl's Prayer

Katherine Mansfield

Grant me the moment, the lovely moment
That I may lean forth to see
The other buds, the other blooms,
The other leaves on the tree:

That I may take into my bosom
The breeze that is like his brother,
But stiller, lighter, whose faint laughter
Echoes the joy of the other.

Above on the blue and white cloud-spaces
There are small clouds at play.
I watch their remote, mysterious play-time
In the other far-away.

Grant I may hear the small birds singing
The song that the silence knows...
(The Light and the Shadow whisper together,
The lovely moment grows,

Ripples into the air like water
Away and away without sound,
And the little girl gets up from her praying
On the cold ground.)

I'm Nobody! Who Are You?

Emily Dickinson

I'm Nobody! Who are you?
Are you — Nobody — too?
Then there's a pair of us!
Dont tell! they'd banish us — you know!

How dreary — to be — Somebody!
How public — like a Frog —
To tell your name — the livelong June —
To an admiring Bog!

We Talked as Girls Do

Emily Dickinson

We talked as Girls do —
Fond, and late —
We speculated fair, on every subject, but the Grave —
Of ours, none affair —

We handled Destinies, as cool —
As we — Disposers — be —
And God, a Quiet Party
To our Authority —

But fondest, dwelt upon Ourself
As we eventual — be —
When Girls to Women, softly raised
We — occupy — Degree —

We parted with a contract
To cherish, and to write
But Heaven made both, impossible
Before another night.

In the Garret

Louisa May Alcott

Four little chests all in a row,
　　Dim with dust, and worn by time,
All fashioned and filled, long ago,
　　By children now in their prime.
Four little keys hung side by side,
　　With faded ribbons, brave and gay,
When fastened there with childish pride,
　　Long ago, on a rainy day.
Four little names, one on each lid,
　　Carved out by a boyish hand,
And underneath, there lieth hid
　　Histories of the happy band
Once playing here, and pausing oft
　　To hear the sweet refrain,
That came and went on the roof aloft,
　　In the falling summer rain.

"Meg" on the first lid, smooth and fair,
　　I look in with loving eyes,
For folded here, with well-known care,
　　A goodly gathering lies—
The record of a peaceful life,
　　Gifts to gentle child and girl,
A bridal gown, lines to a wife,
　　A tiny shoe, a baby curl.

No toys in this first chest remain,
    For all are carried away,
In their old age, to join again
    In another small Meg's play.
Ah, happy mother! well I know
    You hear like a sweet refrain,
Lullabies ever soft and low,
    In the falling summer rain.

"Jo" on the next lid, scratched and worn,
    And within a motley store
Of headless dolls, of school-books torn,
    Birds and beasts that speak no more.
Spoils brought home from the fairy ground
    Only trod by youthful feet,
Dreams of a future never found,
    Memories of a past still sweet;
Half-writ poems, stories wild,
    April letters, warm and cold,
Diaries of a wilful child,
    Hints of a woman early old;
A woman in a lonely home,
    Hearing like a sad refrain,—
"Be worthy love, and love will come,"
    In the falling summer rain.

My "Beth!" the dust is always swept
    From the lid that bears your name,
As if by loving eyes that wept,
    By careful hands that often came.

Death canonized for us one saint,
    Ever less human than divine,
And still we lay, with tender plaint,
    Relics in this household shrine.
The silver bell, so seldom rung,
    The little cap which last she wore,
The fair, dead Catherine that hung
    By angels borne above her door;
The songs she sang, without lament,
    In her prison-house of pain,
Forever are they sweetly blent
    With the falling summer rain.

Upon the last lid's polished field—
    Legend now both fair and true—
A gallant knight bears on his shield,
    "Amy," in letters gold and blue.
Within the snoods that bound her hair,
    Slippers that have danced their last,
Faded flowers laid by with care,
    Fans whose airy toils are past—
Gay valentines all ardent flames,
    Trifles that have borne their part
In girlish hopes, and fears, and shames:
    The record of a maiden heart,
Now learning fairer, truer spells,
    Hearing, like a blithe refrain,
The silver sound of bridal bells
    In the falling summer rain.

Four little chests all in a row,
    Dim with dust, and worn by time,
Four women, taught by weal and woe,
    To love and labor in their prime.
Four sisters, parted for an hour,—
    None lost, one only gone before,
Made by love's immortal power,
    Nearest and dearest evermore.
Oh, when these hidden stores of ours
    Lie open to the Father's sight,
May they be rich in golden hours,—
    Deeds that show fairer for the light.
Lives whose brave music long shall ring
    Like a spirit-stirring strain,
Souls that shall gladly soar and sing
    In the long sunshine after rain.

Everyone Sang

Siegfried Sassoon

Everyone suddenly burst out singing;
And I was filled with such delight
As prisoned birds must find in freedom,
Winging wildly across the white
Orchards and dark-green fields; on—on—and out of sight.

Everyone's voice was suddenly lifted;
And beauty came like the setting sun:
My heart was shaken with tears; and horror
Drifted away . . . O, but Everyone
Was a bird; and the song was wordless; the singing
  will never be done.

ANIMALS

It is possible to discover a new animal every time you visit the zoo, and those creatures represent only a sliver of all the diverse forms of life around the world. From the tiny insect to the towering mammal, there is something marvelous about every type of animal. The grasshopper and the cricket are perfectly in tune with the seasons, the chambered nautilus grows a magnificent spiral shell, and the curious platypus seems to defy all categories by fitting several at once. The following poems capture the different ways that animals manage to amaze and perplex with their unique abilities and traits.

The Duel

Eugene Field

The gingham dog and the calico cat
   Side by side on the table sat;
'T was half-past twelve, and (what do you think!)
Nor one nor t' other had slept a wink!
   The old Dutch clock and the Chinese plate
   Appeared to know as sure as fate
There was going to be a terrible spat.
      (I was n't there; I simply state
      What was told to me by the Chinese plate!)

The gingham dog went "bow-wow-wow!"
And the calico cat replied "mee-ow!"
The air was littered, an hour or so,
With bits of gingham and calico,
   While the old Dutch clock in the chimney place
   Up with its hands before its face,
For it always dreaded a family row!
      (Now mind: I'm only telling you
      What the old Dutch clock declares is true!)

The Chinese plate looked very blue,
And wailed, "Oh, dear! what shall we do!"
But the gingham dog and the calico cat

Wallowed this way and tumbled that,
　　Employing every tooth and claw
　　In the awfullest way you ever saw—
And, oh! how the gingham and calico flew!
　　(Don't fancy I exaggerate—
　　I got my news from the Chinese plate!)

Next morning, where the two had sat
They found no trace of dog or cat;
And some folks think unto this day
That burglars stole that pair away!
　　But the truth about the cat and pup
　　Is this: they ate each other up!
Now what do you really think of that!
　　(The old Dutch clock it told me so,
　　And that is how I came to know.)

The Spider and the Fly

Mary Howitt

"Will you walk into my parlor?" said the Spider to the Fly,
"'T is the prettiest little parlor that ever you did spy;
The way into my parlor is up a winding stair,
And I've many curious things to show when you are there."
"Oh no, no," said the little Fly, "to ask me is in vain,
For who goes up your winding stair can ne'er come down
    again."

"I'm sure you must be weary, dear, with soaring up so high;
Will you rest upon my little bed?" said the Spider to the Fly.
"There are pretty curtains drawn around; the sheets are
    fine and thin,
And if you like to rest awhile, I'll snugly tuck you in!"
"Oh no, no," said the little Fly, "for I've often heard it said,
They never, never wake again, who sleep upon your bed!"

Said the cunning Spider to the Fly, "Dear friend what can
    I do,
To prove the warm affection I've always felt for you?
I have within my pantry, good store of all that's nice;
I'm sure you're very welcome—will you please to take a
    slice?"
"Oh no, no," said the little Fly, "kind sir, that cannot be,
I've heard what's in your pantry, and I do not wish to see!"

"Sweet creature!" said the Spider, "you're witty and you're
      wise,
How handsome are your gauzy wings, how brilliant are your
      eyes!
I've a little looking-glass upon my parlor shelf,
If you'll step in one moment, dear, you shall behold yourself."
"I thank you, gentle sir," she said, "for what you're pleased to
      say,
And bidding you good morning now, I'll call another day."

The Spider turned him round about, and went into his den,
For well he knew the silly Fly would soon come back again:
So he wove a subtle web, in a little corner sly,
And set his table ready, to dine upon the Fly.
Then he came out to his door again, and merrily did sing,
"Come hither, hither, pretty Fly, with the pearl and silver
      wing;
Your robes are green and purple—there's a crest upon your
      head;
Your eyes are like the diamond bright, but mine are dull as
      lead!"

Alas, alas! how very soon this silly little Fly,
Hearing his wily, flattering words, came slowly flitting by;
With buzzing wings she hung aloft, then near and nearer
      drew,
Thinking only of her brilliant eyes, and green and
      purple hue—
Thinking only of her crested head—poor foolish thing!
      At last,

Up jumped the cunning Spider, and fiercely held her fast.
He dragged her up his winding stair, into his dismal den,
Within his little parlor—but she ne'er came out again!

And now dear little children, who may this story read,
To idle, silly flattering words, I pray you ne'er give heed:
Unto an evil counselor, close heart and ear and eye,
And take a lesson from this tale, of the Spider and the Fly.

Upon the Swallow

John Bunyan

This pretty bird, O! how she flies and sings,
But could she do so if she had not wings?
Her wings bespeak my faith, her songs my peace;
When I believe and sing my doubtings cease.

On the Grasshopper and Cricket

John Keats

The poetry of earth is never dead:
   When all the birds are faint with the hot sun,
   And hide in cooling trees, a voice will run
From hedge to hedge about the new-mown mead.
That is the Grasshopper's—he takes the lead
   In summer luxury,—he has never done
   With his delights; for when tired out with fun,
He rests at ease beneath some pleasant weed.
The poetry of earth is ceasing never:
   On a lone winter evening, when the frost
      Has wrought a silence, from the stove there shrills
The Cricket's song, in warmth increasing ever,
   And seems to one in drowsiness half lost,
      The Grasshopper's among some grassy hills.

The Little Turtle

Vachel Lindsay

There was a little turtle.
He lived in a box.
He swam in a puddle.
He climbed on the rocks.

He snapped at a mosquito.
He snapped at a flea.
He snapped at a minnow.
And he snapped at me.

He caught the mosquito.
He caught the flea.
He caught the minnow.
But he didn't catch me.

A Noiseless Patient Spider

Walt Whitman

A noiseless patient spider,
I mark'd where on a little promontory it stood isolated,
Mark'd how to explore the vacant vast surrounding,
It launch'd forth filament, filament, filament, out of itself,
Ever unreeling them, ever tirelessly speeding them.

And you O my soul where you stand,
Surrounded, detached, in measureless oceans of space,
Ceaselessly musing, venturing, throwing, seeking the
    spheres to connect them,
Till the bridge you will need be form'd, till the ductile
    anchor hold,
Till the gossamer thread you fling catch somewhere,
    O my soul.

Old Pond

Bashō

Old pond—
A frog leaps in—
Water's sound.

At the Zoo

William Makepeace Thackeray

First I saw the white bear, then I saw the black,
Then I saw the camel with a hump upon his back.
Then I saw the gray wolf, with mutton in his maw;
Then I saw the wombat waddle in the straw;
Then I saw the elephant with his waving trunk,
Then I saw the monkeys—mercy, how unpleasantly they—
     smelt!

The Kitten and Falling Leaves

William Wordsworth

That way look, my Infant, lo!
What a pretty baby-show!
See the Kitten on the wall,
Sporting with the leaves that fall,
Withered leaves—one—two—and three—
From the lofty elder-tree!
Through the calm and frosty air
Of this morning bright and fair,
Eddying round and round they sink
Softly, slowly: one might think,
From the motions that are made,
Every little leaf conveyed
Sylph or Faery hither tending,—
To this lower world descending,
Each invisible and mute,
In his wavering parachute.
—But the Kitten, how she starts,
Crouches, stretches, paws, and darts!
First at one, and then its fellow
Just as light and just as yellow;
There are many now—now one—
Now they stop and there are none.
What intenseness of desire
In her upward eye of fire!
With a tiger-leap half-way

Now she meets the coming prey,
Lets it go as fast, and then
Has it in her power again:
Now she works with three or four,
Like an Indian conjurer;
Quick as he in feats of art,
Far beyond in joy of heart.
Were her antics played in the eye
Of a thousand standers-by,
Clapping hands with shout and stare,
What would little Tabby care
For the plaudits of the crowd?
Over happy to be proud,
Over wealthy in the treasure
Of her own exceeding pleasure!

   'Tis a pretty baby-treat;
Nor, I deem, for me unmeet;
Here, for neither Babe nor me,
Other play-mate can I see.
Of the countless living things,
That with stir of feet and wings
(In the sun or under shade,
Upon bough or grassy blade)
And with busy revelings,
Chirp and song, and murmurings,
Made this orchard's narrow space,
And this vale so blithe a place;
Multitudes are swept away
Never more to breathe the day:

Some are sleeping; some in bands
Traveled into distant lands;
Others slunk to moor and wood,
Far from human neighborhood;
And, among the Kinds that keep
With us closer fellowship,
With us openly abide,
All have laid their mirth aside.

  Where is he that giddy Sprite,
Blue-cap, with his colors bright,
Who was blest as bird could be,
Feeding in the apple-tree:
Made such wanton spoil and rout,
Turning blossoms inside out;
Hung—head pointing towards the ground—
Fluttered, perched, into a round
Bound himself, and then unbound;
Lithest, gaudiest Harlequin!
Prettiest Tumbler ever seen!
Light of heart and light of limb;
What is now become of Him?
Lambs, that through the mountains went
Frisking, bleating merriment,
When the year was in its prime,
They are sobered by this time.
If you look to vale or hill,
If you listen, all is still,
Save a little neighboring rill,
That from out the rocky ground

Strikes a solitary sound.
Vainly glitter hill and plain;
And the air is calm in vain;
Vainly Morning spreads the lure
Of a sky serene and pure;
Creature none can she decoy
Into open sign of joy:
Is it that they have a fear
Of the dreary season near?
Or that other pleasures be
Sweeter even than gaiety?

    Yet, whate'er enjoyments dwell
In the impenetrable cell
Of the silent heart which Nature
Furnishes to every creature;
Whatsoe'er we feel and know
Too sedate for outward show,
Such a light of gladness breaks,
Pretty Kitten! from thy freaks,—
Spreads with such a living grace
O'er my little Dora's face;
Yes, the sight so stirs and charms
Thee, Baby, laughing in my arms,
That almost I could repine
That your transports are not mine,
That I do not wholly fare
Even as ye do, thoughtless pair!
And I will have my careless season
Spite of melancholy reason,

Will walk through life in such a way
That, when time brings on decay,
Now and then I may possess
Hours of perfect gladsomeness.
—Pleased by any random toy;
By a kitten's busy joy,
Or an infant's laughing eye
Sharing in the ecstasy;
I would fare like that or this
Find my wisdom in my bliss;
Keep the sprightly soul awake,
And have faculties to take,
Even from things by sorrow wrought,
Matter for a jocund thought,
Spite of care, and spite of grief,
To gambol with Life's falling Leaf.

The Chambered Nautilus

Oliver Wendell Holmes

This is the ship of pearl, which, poets feign,
    Sails the unshadowed main,—
    The venturous bark that flings
On the sweet summer wind its purpled wings
In gulfs enchanted, where the siren sings,
    And coral reefs lie bare,
Where the cold sea-maids rise to sun their streaming hair.

Its webs of living gauze no more unfurl;
    Wrecked is the ship of pearl!
    And every chambered cell,
Where its dim dreaming life was wont to dwell,
As the frail tenant shaped his growing shell,
    Before thee lies revealed,—
Its irised ceiling rent, its sunless crypt unsealed!

Year after year beheld the silent toil
    That spread his lustrous coil;
    Still, as the spiral grew,
He left the past year's dwelling for the new,
Stole with soft step its shining archway through,
    Built up its idle door,
Stretched in his last-found home, and knew the old no more.

Thanks for the heavenly message brought by thee,
    Child of the wandering sea,
    Cast from her lap, forlorn!
From thy dead lips a clearer note is born
Than ever Triton blew from wreathèd horn!
    While on mine ear it rings,
Through the deep caves of thought I hear a voice that
    sings:—

Build thee more stately mansions, O my soul,
    As the swift seasons roll!
    Leave thy low-vaulted past!
Let each new temple, nobler than the last,
Shut thee from heaven with a dome more vast,
    Till thou at length art free,
Leaving thine outgrown shell by life's unresting sea!

The Wild Swans at Coole

William Butler Yeats

The trees are in their autumn beauty,
The woodland paths are dry,
Under the October twilight the water
Mirrors a still sky;
Upon the brimming water among the stones
Are nine and fifty swans.

The nineteenth Autumn has come upon me
Since I first made my count;
I saw, before I had well finished,
All suddenly mount
And scatter wheeling in great broken rings
Upon their clamorous wings.

I have looked upon those brilliant creatures,
And now my heart is sore.
All's changed since I, hearing at twilight,
The first time on this shore,
The bell-beat of their wings above my head,
Trod with a lighter tread.

Unwearied still, lover by lover,
They paddle in the cold,
Companionable streams or climb the air;
Their hearts have not grown old;
Passion or conquest, wander where they will,
Attend upon them still.

But now they drift on the still water
Mysterious, beautiful;
Among what rushes will they build,
By what lake's edge or pool
Delight men's eyes, when I awake some day
To find they have flown away?

The Platypus

Oliver Herford

My child, the Duck-billed Platypus
A sad example sets for us.
From him we learn how Indecision
Of character provokes Derision.
This vacillating thing, you see,
Could not decide which he would be—
Fish, Flesh or Fowl,—and chose all three.
The scientists were sorely vexed,
To classify him so perplexed
Their brains that they with rage at bay
Called him a horrid name one day,
A name that baffles, frights and shocks us,
Ornithorynchus Paradoxus.

Ode on the Death of a Favorite Cat, Drowned in a Tub of Gold Fishes

Thomas Gray

'Twas on a lofty vase's side,
Where China's gayest art had dy'd
   The azure flowers, that blow;
Demurest of the tabby kind,
The pensive Selima reclin'd,
   Gazed on the lake below.

Her conscious tail her joy declar'd;
The fair round face, the snowy beard,
   The velvet of her paws,
Her coat, that with the tortoise vies,
Her ears of jet, and emerald eyes,
   She saw; and purr'd applause.

Still had she gaz'd; but 'midst the tide
Two angel forms were seen to glide,
   The Genii of the stream:
Their scaly armor's Tyrian hue
Thro' richest purple to the view
   Betray'd a golden gleam.

The hapless Nymph with wonder saw:
A whisker first and then a claw,
    With many an ardent wish,
She stretch'd in vain to reach the prize.
What female heart can gold despise?
    What Cat's averse to fish?

Presumptuous Maid! with looks intent
Again she stretch'd, again she bent,
    Nor knew the gulf between.
(Malignant Fate sat by, and smil'd)
The slipp'ry verge her feet beguil'd,
    She tumbled headlong in.

Eight times emerging from the flood
She mew'd to ev'ry watry God,
    Some speedy aid to send.
No Dolphin came, no Nereid stirr'd:
Nor cruel *Tom,* nor *Susan* heard.
    A Fav'rite has no friend!

From hence, ye Beauties, undeceiv'd,
Know, one false step is ne'er retriev'd,
    And be with caution bold.
Not all that tempts your wand'ring eyes
And heedless hearts, is lawful prize;
    Nor all, that glisters, gold.

The Cat and the Moon

William Butler Yeats

The cat went here and there
And the moon spun round like a top,
And the nearest kin of the moon
The creeping cat looked up.
Black Minnaloushe stared at the moon,
For wander and wail as he would
The pure cold light in the sky
Troubled his animal blood.
Minnaloushe runs in the grass,
Lifting his delicate feet.
Do you dance, Minnaloushe, do you dance?
When two close kindred meet
What better than call a dance,
Maybe the moon may learn,
Tired of that courtly fashion,
A new dance turn.
Minnaloushe creeps through the grass
From moonlit place to place,
The sacred moon overhead
Has taken a new phase.
Does Minnaloushe know that his pupils
Will pass from change to change,
And that from round to crescent,
From crescent to round they range?

Minnaloushe creeps through the grass
Alone, important and wise,
And lifts to the changing moon
His changing eyes.

To Flush, My Dog

Elizabeth Barrett Browning

Loving friend, the gift of one,
Who, her own true faith, hath run,
   Through thy lower nature;
Be my benediction said
With my hand upon thy head,
   Gentle fellow-creature!

Like a lady's ringlets brown,
Flow thy silken ears adown
   Either side demurely,
Of thy silver-suited breast
Shining out from all the rest
   Of thy body purely.

Darkly brown thy body is,
Till the sunshine, striking this,
   Alchemize its dullness,—
When the sleek curls manifold
Flash all over into gold,
   With a burnished fullness.

Underneath my stroking hand,
Startled eyes of hazel bland
   Kindling, growing larger,—
Up thou leapest with a spring,

Full of prank and curvetting,
    Leaping like a charger.

Leap! thy broad tail waves a light;
Leap! thy slender feet are bright,
    Canopied in fringes.
Leap—those tasseled ears of thine
Flicker strangely, fair and fine,
    Down their golden inches

Yet, my pretty sportive friend,
Little is 't to such an end
    That I praise thy rareness!
Other dogs may be thy peers
Haply in these drooping ears,
    And this glossy fairness.

But of *thee* it shall be said,
This dog watched beside a bed
    Day and night unweary,—
Watched within a curtained room,
Where no sunbeam brake the gloom
    Round the sick and dreary.

Roses, gathered for a vase,
In that chamber died apace,
    Beam and breeze resigning—
This dog only, waited on,
Knowing that when light is gone,
    Love remains for shining.

Other dogs in thymy dew
Tracked the hares and followed through
    Sunny moor or meadow—
This dog only, crept and crept
Next a languid cheek that slept,
    Sharing in the shadow.

Other dogs of loyal cheer
Bounded at the whistle clear,
    Up the woodside hieing—
This dog only, watched in reach
Of a faintly uttered speech,
    Or a louder sighing.

And if one or two quick tears
Dropped upon his glossy ears,
    Or a sigh came double,—
Up he sprang in eager haste,
Fawning, fondling, breathing fast,
    In a tender trouble,

And this dog was satisfied,
If a pale thin hand would glide,
    Down his dewlaps sloping,—
Which he pushed his nose within,
After,—platforming his chin
    On the palm left open.

This dog, if a friendly voice
Call him now to blyther choice
   Than such chamber-keeping,
"Come out!" praying from the door,—
Presseth backward as before,
   Up against me leaping.

Therefore to this dog will I,
Tenderly not scornfully,
   Render praise and favor!
With my hand upon his head,
Is my benediction said
   Therefore, and for ever.

And because he loves me so,
Better than his kind will do
   Often, man or woman,—
Give I back more love again
Than dogs often take of men,—
   Leaning from my Human.

Blessings on thee, dog of mine,
Pretty collars make thee fine,
   Sugared milk make fat thee!
Pleasures wag on in thy tail—
Hands of gentle motion fail
   Nevermore, to pat thee!

Downy pillow take thy head,
Silken coverlid bestead,
  Sunshine help thy sleeping!
No fly's buzzing wake thee up—
No man break thy purple cup,
  Set for drinking deep in.

Whiskered cats arointed flee—
Sturdy stoppers keep from thee
  Cologne distillations;
Nuts lie in thy path for stones,
And thy feast-day macaroons
  Turn to daily rations!

Mock I thee, in wishing weal?—
Tears are in my eyes to feel
  Thou art made so straightly,
Blessing needs must straighten too,—
Little canst thou joy or do,
  Thou who lovest *greatly*.

Yet be blessed to the height
Of all good and all delight
  Pervious to thy nature,—
Only *loved* beyond that line,
With a love that answers thine,
  Loving fellow-creature!

NURSERY RHYMES

Nursery rhymes were originally handed down orally, often through song, and for the most part no one kept track of who created each poem. Even though many nursery rhymes were inspired by historic or political events, few people know their true origins today. And yet somehow these poems have managed to survive from one generation to the next to become part of the fabric of our culture. Perhaps their longevity lies in the fact that they are among the most fun poems to memorize and read aloud. In fact, the first words ever recorded on a machine were four lines from "Mary Had a Little Lamb," spoken by Thomas Edison into his groundbreaking invention, the phonograph, in 1877.

What Are Little Girls Made Of?

Anonymous

What are little girls made of?
What are little girls made of?
  Sugar and spice
  And all that's nice,
That's what little girls are made of.

What are little boys made of?
What are little boys made of?
  Frogs and snails
  And puppy-dogs' tails,
That's what little boys are made of.

There Was a Little Girl

Henry Wadsworth Longfellow

There was a little girl,
Who had a little curl,
Right in the middle of her forehead.
When she was good,
She was very good indeed,
But when she was bad she was horrid.

Monday's Child

Anonymous

Monday's child is fair of face,
Tuesday's child is full of grace,
Wednesday's child is full of woe,
Thursday's child has far to go,
Friday's child is loving and giving,
Saturday's child works hard for his living,
And the child that is born on the Sabbath day
Is bonny and blithe, and good and gay.

The Star

Jane Taylor

Twinkle, twinkle, little star,
How I wonder what you are!
Up above the world so high,
Like a diamond in the sky.

When the blazing sun is gone,
When he nothing shines upon,
Then you show your little light,
Twinkle, twinkle, all the night.

Then the traveler in the dark,
Thanks you for your tiny spark,
He could not see which way to go,
If you did not twinkle so.

In the dark blue sky you keep,
And often through my curtains peep,
For you never shut your eye,
Till the sun is in the sky.

As your bright and tiny spark,
Lights the traveler in the dark,—
Though I know not what you are,
Twinkle, twinkle, little star.

Little Miss Muffet

Anonymous

Little Miss Muffet
Sat on a tuffet,
Eating her curds and whey;
There came a big spider,
Who sat down beside her
And frightened Miss Muffet away.

Mary Had a Little Lamb

Sarah Josepha Hale

Mary had a little lamb,
   Its fleece was white as snow;
And everywhere that Mary went
   The lamb was sure to go.

It followed her to school one day,
   That was against the rule;
It made the children laugh and play
   To see a lamb at school.

And so the teacher turned it out,
   But still it lingered near,
And waited patiently about
   Till Mary did appear.

Why does the lamb love Mary so?
   The eager children cry;
Why, Mary loves the lamb, you know,
   The teacher did reply.

Mary, Mary, Quite Contrary

Anonymous

Mary, Mary, quite contrary,
    How does your garden grow?
With silver bells and cockle shells,
    And pretty maids all in a row.

Three Little Kittens, They Lost Their Mittens

Anonymous

Three little kittens, they lost their mittens,
    And they began to cry,
"Oh, mother dear, we sadly fear
    That we have lost our mittens."
"What! lost your mittens, you naughty kittens!
    Then you shall have no pie."
        "Mee-ow, mee-ow, mee-ow."
        "No, you shall have no pie."

The three little kittens, they found their mittens,
    And they began to cry,
"Oh, mother dear, see here, see here,
    For we have found our mittens."
"Put on your mittens, you silly kittens,
    And you shall have some pie."
        "Purr-r, purr-r, purr-r,
        Oh, let us have some pie."

The three little kittens put on their mittens,
    And soon ate up the pie;
"Oh, mother dear, we greatly fear
    That we have soiled our mittens."

"What! soiled your mittens, you naughty kittens!"
    Then they began to sigh.
    "Mee-ow, mee-ow, mee-ow."
    Then they began to sigh.

The three little kittens, they washed their mittens,
    And hung them out to dry;
"Oh! mother dear, do you not hear
    That we have washed our mittens?"
"What! washed your mittens, then you're good kittens,
    But I smell a rat close by."
    "Mee-ow, mee-ow, mee-ow.
    We smell a rat close by."

Jack and Jill

Anonymous

Jack and Jill went up the hill
　To fetch a pail of water;
Jack fell down and broke his crown,
　And Jill came tumbling after.

Up Jack got, and home did trot,
　As fast as he could caper,
To old Dame Dob, who patched his nob
　With vinegar and brown paper.

Little Bo-Peep

Anonymous

Little Bo-Peep has lost her sheep,
And can't tell where to find them;
Leave them alone, and they'll come home,
Bringing their tails behind them.

Little Bo-Peep fell fast asleep,
And dreamt she heard them bleating;
But when she awoke, she found it a joke,
For they were still all fleeting.

Then up she took her little crook,
Determined for to find them;
She found them indeed, but it made her heart bleed,
For they'd left their tails behind them.

It happened one day, as Bo-Peep did stray
Into a meadow hard by,
There she espied their tails, side by side,
All hung on a tree to dry.

She heaved a sigh and wiped her eye,
And over the hillocks she raced;
And tried what she could, as a shepherdess should,
That each tail be properly placed.

The Itsy Bitsy Spider

Anonymous

The itsy bitsy spider went up the water spout.
Down came the rain, and washed the spider out.
Out came the sun, and dried up all the rain,
And the itsy bitsy spider went up the spout again.

Ladybird, Ladybird

Anonymous

Ladybird, ladybird,
   Fly away home,
Your house is on fire
   And your children all gone;

All except one
   And that's little Ann
And she has crept under
   The warming pan.

Fuzzy Wuzzy Was a Bear

Anonymous

Fuzzy Wuzzy was a bear.
Fuzzy Wuzzy had no hair.
Fuzzy Wuzzy wasn't fuzzy, was he?

It's Raining, It's Pouring

Anonymous

It's raining, it's pouring,
The old man's snoring;
He got into bed
And bumped his head
And couldn't get up in the morning.

LIMERICKS AND TONGUE TWISTERS

Even if you've never heard a limerick before, it doesn't take long to see a pattern in this type of poetry. They all sound alike, but there is plenty of room for variety, and the wittier or more nonsensical the better. No one knows exactly where limericks originated, though a popular theory is that they began as a party game where guests made up verses on the spot. Perhaps you'll be inspired to create a limerick of your own after reading the following poems! Unlike limericks, tongue twisters have no distinct rhyme scheme. They are designed to be read aloud as fast as possible. The challenge is to reach the end of a tongue twister without stumbling over a tricky alliteration or repetition, though sometimes it can be funnier if you do.

There was a Young Lady Whose Eyes

Edward Lear

There was a Young Lady whose eyes
Were unique as to color and size;
When she opened them wide, people all turned aside,
And started away in surprise.

There Was a Young Lady of Dorking

Edward Lear

There was a Young Lady of Dorking,
Who bought a large bonnet for walking;
But its color and size so bedazzled her eyes,
That she very soon went back to Dorking.

There Was a Young Lady of Portugal

Edward Lear

There was a Young Lady of Portugal,
Whose ideas were excessively nautical;
She climbed up a tree to examine the sea,
But declared she would never leave Portugal.

There Was a Young Lady Whose Chin

Edward Lear

There was a Young Lady whose chin,
Resembled the point of a pin;
So she had it made sharp, and purchased a harp,
And played several tunes with her chin.

There Once Was a Man from Nantucket

Anonymous

There once was a man from Nantucket,
Who kept all his cash in a bucket,
    But his daughter, named Nan,
    Ran away with a man,
And as for the bucket, Nantucket.

I Wish That My Room Had a Floor!

Gelett Burgess

I Wish that my Room had a Floor!
I don't so Much Care for a Door,
  But this Crawling Around
  Without Touching the Ground
Is Getting to be Quite a Bore!

Peter Piper picked a peck of pickled pepper;
A peck of pickled pepper Peter Piper picked;
If Peter Piper picked a peck of pickled pepper,
Where's the peck of pickled pepper Peter Piper picked?

Betty Botter bought some butter,
But, she said, the butter's bitter;
If I put it in my batter
It will make my batter bitter,
But a bit of better butter
Will make my batter better.
So she bought a bit of butter
Better than her bitter butter,
And she put it in her batter
And the batter was not bitter.
So t'was better Betty Botter bought a bit of better butter.

A flea and a fly flew up in a flue.
Said the flea, "Let us fly!"
Said the fly, "Let us flee!"
So they flew through a flaw in the flue.

A tutor who tooted the flute
Tried to tutor two tooters to toot.
  Said the two to the tutor,
  "Is it harder to toot or
To tutor two tooters to toot?"

How much wood could a woodchuck chuck
If a woodchuck could chuck wood?
As much wood as a woodchuck would,
If a woodchuck could chuck wood.

She sells seashells by the seashore.
    The shells she sells are surely seashells.
    So if she sells shells on the seashore,
    I'm sure she sells seashore shells.

FUN AND
NONSENSE

Who ever heard of a purple cow, or falling up rather than down?
Everything is a little out of the ordinary in the following poems. A
brave little girl turns a mean witch into a glass of milk, an elephant
tries to use a telephone, and an owl and a pussycat dance under
the moon. Some of these pieces are just plain nonsense and
others are particularly fun to read aloud, like "The Bells" and
"Beautiful Soup." You'll probably find yourself giggling, chuckling,
or even snorting while reading this hilarious assortment.

Laughing Song

William Blake

When the green woods laugh with the voice of joy
And the dimpling stream runs laughing by,
When the air does laugh with our merry wit,
And the green hill laughs with the noise of it,

When the meadows laugh with lively green
And the grasshopper laughs in the merry scene,
When Mary and Susan and Emily
With their sweet round mouths sing "Ha, Ha, He,"

When the painted birds laugh in the shade
Where our table with cherries and nuts is spread,
Come live & be merry and join with me,
To sing the sweet chorus of "Ha, Ha, He."

Adventures of Isabel

Ogden Nash

Isabel met an enormous bear,
Isabel, Isabel, didn't care;
The bear was hungry, the bear was ravenous,
The bear's big mouth was cruel and cavernous.
The bear said, Isabel, glad to meet you,
How do, Isabel, now I'll eat you!
Isabel, Isabel, didn't worry,
Isabel didn't scream or scurry.
She washed her hands and she straightened her hair up,
Then Isabel quietly ate the bear up.

Once in a night as black as pitch
Isabel met a wicked old witch.
The witch's face was cross and wrinkled,
The witch's gums with teeth were sprinkled.
Ho ho, Isabel! the old witch crowed,
I'll turn you into an ugly toad!
Isabel, Isabel, didn't worry,
Isabel didn't scream or scurry,
She showed no rage and she showed no rancor,
But she turned the witch into milk and drank her.

Isabel met a hideous giant,
Isabel continued self-reliant.
The giant was hairy, the giant was horrid,
He had one eye in the middle of his forehead.
Good morning Isabel, the giant said,
I'll grind your bones to make my bread.
Isabel, Isabel, didn't worry,
Isabel didn't scream or scurry.
She nibbled the zwieback that she always fed off,
And when it was gone, she cut the giant's head off.

Isabel met a troublesome doctor,
He punched and he poked till he really shocked her.
The doctor's talk was of coughs and chills
And the doctor's satchel bulged with pills.
The doctor said unto Isabel,
Swallow this, it will make you well.
Isabel, Isabel, didn't worry,
Isabel didn't scream or scurry.
She took those pills from the pill concocter,
And Isabel calmly cured the doctor.

The Sniffle

Ogden Nash

In spite of her sniffle,
Isabel's chiffle.
Some girls with a sniffle
Would be weepy and tiffle;
They would look awful,
Like a rained-on waffle,
But Isabel's chiffle
In spite of her sniffle.
Her nose is more red
With a cold in her head,
But then, to be sure,
Her eyes are bluer.
Some girls with a snuffle,
Their tempers are uffle,
But when Isabel's snivelly
She's snivelly civilly,
And when she is snuffly
She's perfectly luffly.

The Bells

Edgar Allan Poe

1

Hear the sledges with the bells—
Silver bells!
What a world of merriment their melody foretells!
How they tinkle, tinkle, tinkle,
In the icy air of night!
While the stars that oversprinkle
All the heavens, seem to twinkle
With a crystalline delight;
Keeping time, time, time,
In a sort of Runic rhyme,
To the tintinnabulation that so musically wells
From the bells, bells, bells, bells,
Bells, bells, bells—
From the jingling and the tinkling of the bells.

2

Hear the mellow wedding bells,
Golden bells!
What a world of happiness their harmony foretells!
Through the balmy air of night
How they ring out their delight!
From the molten-golden notes,
And all in tune,
What a liquid ditty floats

To the turtle-dove that listens, while she gloats
On the moon!
Oh, from out the sounding cells,
What a gush of euphony voluminously wells!
How it swells!
How it dwells
On the Future! how it tells
Of the rapture that impels
To the swinging and the ringing
Of the bells, bells, bells,
Of the bells, bells, bells, bells,
Bells, bells, bells—
To the rhyming and the chiming of the bells!

3

Hear the loud alarum bells—
Brazen bells!
What a tale of terror, now, their turbulency tells!
In the startled ear of night
How they scream out their affright!
Too much horrified to speak,
They can only shriek, shriek,
Out of tune,
In a clamorous appealing to the mercy of the fire,
In a mad expostulation with the deaf and frantic fire,
Leaping higher, higher, higher,
With a desperate desire,
And a resolute endeavor,
Now—now to sit or never,
By the side of the pale-faced moon.

Oh, the bells, bells, bells!
What a tale their terror tells
            Of Despair!
How they clang, and clash, and roar!
What a horror they outpour
On the bosom of the palpitating air!
        Yet the ear it fully knows,
            By the twanging,
            And the clanging,
        How the danger ebbs and flows:
Yet the ear distinctly tells,
            In the jangling,
            And the wrangling,
        How the danger sinks and swells,
By the sinking or the swelling in the anger of the bells—
            Of the bells—
    Of the bells, bells, bells, bells,
        Bells, bells, bells—
    In the clamor and the clanger of the bells!

                    4
    Hear the tolling of the bells—
            Iron bells!
What a world of solemn thought their monody compels!
        In the silence of the night,
        How we shiver with affright
    At the melancholy menace of their tone!
        For every sound that floats
        From the rust within their throats
            Is a groan.

And the people—ah, the people—
They that dwell up in the steeple,
    All alone,
And who, tolling, tolling, tolling,
  In that muffled monotone,
Feel a glory in so rolling
  On the human heart a stone—
They are neither man nor woman—
They are neither brute nor human—
    They are Ghouls:
  And their king it is who tolls;
  And he rolls, rolls, rolls,
    Rolls
     A paean from the bells!
And his merry bosom swells
  With the paean of the bells!
And he dances, and he yells;
Keeping time, time, time,
In a sort of Runic rhyme,
  To the paean of the bells—
    Of the bells:
Keeping time, time, time,
In a sort of Runic rhyme,
  To the throbbing of the bells—
Of the bells, bells, bells—
  To the sobbing of the bells;
Keeping time, time, time,
  As he knells, knells, knells,
In a happy Runic rhyme,
  To the rolling of the bells—

Of the bells, bells, bells:
     To the tolling of the bells,
 Of the bells, bells, bells, bells—
     Bells, bells, bells—
To the moaning and the groaning of the bells.

A Visit from St. Nicholas

Clement Clarke Moore

'Twas the night before Christmas, when all through the
    house
Not a creature was stirring, not even a mouse;
The stockings were hung by the chimney with care,
In hopes that St. Nicholas soon would be there;
The children were nestled all snug in their beds,
While visions of sugar-plums danced in their heads;
And mamma in her 'kerchief, and I in my cap,
Had just settled our brains for a long winter's nap—
When out on the lawn there arose such a clatter,
I sprang from my bed to see what was the matter.
Away to the window I flew like a flash,
Tore open the shutters, and threw up the sash.
The moon, on the breast of the new-fallen snow,
Gave the lustre of midday to objects below;
When, what to my wondering eyes should appear,
But a miniature sleigh and eight tiny reindeer,
With a little old driver, so lively and quick,
I knew in a moment it must be St. Nick.
More rapid than eagles his coursers they came,
And he whistled, and shouted, and called them by name:
"Now, Dasher! now, Dancer! now, Prancer and Vixen!
On, Comet! on, Cupid! on, Donder and Blitzen!
To the top of the porch! to the top of the wall!

Now dash away! dash away! dash away all!"
As dry leaves that before the wild hurricane fly,
When they meet with an obstacle, mount to the sky;
So up to the house-top the coursers they flew
With the sleigh full of toys, and St. Nicholas too.
And then, in a twinkling, I heard on the roof
The prancing and pawing of each little hoof—
As I drew in my head, and was turning around,
Down the chimney St. Nicholas came with a bound.
He was dressed all in fur, from his head to his foot,
And his clothes were all tarnished with ashes and soot;
A bundle of toys he had flung on his back,
And he looked like a peddler just opening his pack.
His eyes—how they twinkled; his dimples, how merry!
His cheeks were like roses, his nose like a cherry!
His droll little mouth was drawn up like a bow,
And the beard of his chin was as white as the snow;
The stump of a pipe he held tight in his teeth,
And the smoke it encircled his head like a wreath;
He had a broad face and a little round belly
That shook, when he laughed, like a bowl full of jelly.
He was chubby and plump, a right jolly old elf,
And I laughed when I saw him, in spite of myself;
A wink of his eye and a twist of his head
Soon gave me to know I had nothing to dread;
He spoke not a word, but went straight to his work,
And filled all the stockings; then turned with a jerk,
And laying his finger aside of his nose,
And giving a nod, up the chimney he rose;

He sprang to his sleigh, to his team gave a whistle,
And away they all flew like the down of a thistle.
But I heard him exclaim, ere he drove out of sight,
"Happy Christmas to all, and to all a good night!"

Sarah Cynthia Sylvia Stout Would Not Take the Garbage Out

Shel Silverstein

Sarah Cynthia Sylvia Stout
Would not take the garbage out!
She'd scour the pots and scrape the pans,
Candy the yams and spice the hams,
And though her daddy would scream and shout,
She simply would not take the garbage out.
And so it piled up to the ceilings:
Coffee grounds, potato peelings,
Brown bananas, rotten peas,
Chunks of sour cottage cheese.
It filled the can, it covered the floor,
It cracked the window and blocked the door
With bacon rinds and chicken bones,
Drippy ends of ice cream cones,
Prune pits, peach pits, orange peel,
Gloppy glumps of cold oatmeal,
Pizza crusts and withered greens,
Soggy beans and tangerines,
Crusts of black burned buttered toast,
Gristly bits of beefy roasts...
The garbage rolled on down the hall,
It raised the roof, it broke the wall...
Greasy napkins, cookie crumbs,
Globs of gooey bubble gum,

Cellophane from green baloney,
Rubbery blubbery macaroni,
Peanut butter, caked and dry,
Curdled milk and crusts of pie,
Moldy melons, dried-up mustard,
Eggshells mixed with lemon custard,
Cold french fries and rancid meat,
Yellow lumps of Cream of Wheat.
At last the garbage reached so high
That finally it touched the sky.
And all the neighbors moved away,
And none of her friends would come to play.
And finally Sarah Cynthia Stout said,
"OK, I'll take the garbage out!"
But then, of course, it was too late...
The garbage reached across the state,
From New York to the Golden Gate.
And there, in the garbage she did hate,
Poor Sarah met an awful fate,
That I cannot right now relate
Because the hour is much too late.
But children, remember Sarah Stout
And always take the garbage out!

Falling Up

Shel Silverstein

I tripped on my shoelace
And I fell up—
Up to the roof tops,
Up over the town,
Up past the tree tops,
Up over the mountains,
Up where the colors
Blend into the sounds.
But it got me so dizzy
When I looked around,
I got sick to my stomach
And I threw down.

The Walrus and the Carpenter

Lewis Carroll

The sun was shining on the sea,
    Shining with all his might:
He did his very best to make
    The billows smooth and bright—
And this was odd, because it was
    The middle of the night.

The moon was shining sulkily,
    Because she thought the sun
Had got no business to be there
    After the day was done—
"It's very rude of him," she said,
    "To come and spoil the fun!"

The sea was wet as wet could be,
    The sands were dry as dry.
You could not see a cloud, because
    No cloud was in the sky:
No birds were flying overhead—
    There were no birds to fly.

The Walrus and the Carpenter
    Were walking close at hand;
They wept like anything to see
    Such quantities of sand:

"If this were only cleared away,"
    They said, "it *would* be grand!"

"If seven maids with seven mops
    Swept it for half a year,
Do you suppose," the Walrus said,
    "That they could get it clear?"
"I doubt it," said the Carpenter,
    And shed a bitter tear.

"O Oysters, come and walk with us!"
    The Walrus did beseech.
"A pleasant walk, a pleasant talk,
    Along the briny beach:
We cannot do with more than four,
    To give a hand to each."

The eldest Oyster looked at him,
    But never a word he said:
The eldest Oyster winked his eye,
    And shook his heavy head—
Meaning to say he did not choose
    To leave the oyster-bed.

But four young Oysters hurried up,
    All eager for the treat:
Their coats were brushed, their faces washed,
    Their shoes were clean and neat—
And this was odd, because, you know,
    They hadn't any feet.

Four other Oysters followed them,
    And yet another four;
And thick and fast they came at last,
    And more, and more, and more—
All hopping through the frothy waves,
    And scrambling to the shore.

The Walrus and the Carpenter
    Walked on a mile or so,
And then they rested on a rock
    Conveniently low:
And all the little Oysters stood
    And waited in a row.

"The time has come," the Walrus said,
    "To talk of many things:
Of shoes—and ships—and sealing-wax—
    Of cabbages—and kings—
And why the sea is boiling hot—
    And whether pigs have wings."

"But wait a bit," the Oysters cried,
    "Before we have our chat;
For some of us are out of breath,
    And all of us are fat!"
"No hurry!" said the Carpenter.
    They thanked him much for that.

"A loaf of bread," the Walrus said,
    "Is what we chiefly need:
Pepper and vinegar besides
    Are very good indeed—
Now if you're ready, Oysters dear,
    We can begin to feed."

"But not on us!" the Oysters cried,
    Turning a little blue.
"After such kindness, that would be
    A dismal thing to do!"
"The night is fine," the Walrus said.
    "Do you admire the view?

"It was so kind of you to come!
    And you are very nice!"
The Carpenter said nothing but
    "Cut us another slice:
I wish you were not quite so deaf—
    I've had to ask you twice!"

"It seems a shame," the Walrus said,
    "To play them such a trick,
After we've brought them out so far,
    And made them trot so quick!"
The Carpenter said nothing but
    "The butter's spread too thick!"

"I weep for you," the Walrus said:
   "I deeply sympathize."
With sobs and tears he sorted out
   Those of the largest size,
Holding his pocket-handkerchief
   Before his streaming eyes.

"O Oysters," said the Carpenter,
   "You've had a pleasant run!
Shall we be trotting home again?"
   But answer came there none—
And this was scarcely odd, because
   They'd eaten every one.

Beautiful Soup

Lewis Carroll

Beautiful Soup, so rich and green,
Waiting in a hot tureen!
Who for such dainties would not stoop?
Soup of the evening, beautiful Soup!
Soup of the evening, beautiful Soup!
    Beau—ootiful Soo—oop!
    Beau—ootiful Soo—oop!
Soo—oop of the e—e—evening,
    Beautiful, beautiful Soup!

Beautiful Soup! Who cares for fish,
Game, or any other dish?
Who would not give all else for two p
ennyworth only of beautiful Soup?
Pennyworth only of beautiful Soup?
    Beau—ootiful Soo—oop!
    Beau—ootiful Soo—oop!
Soo—oop of the e—e—evening,
    Beautiful, beauti—FUL SOUP!

Matilda,

WHO TOLD LIES, AND WAS BURNED TO DEATH.

Hilaire Belloc

Matilda told such Dreadful Lies,
It made one Gasp and Stretch one's Eyes;
Her Aunt, who, from her Earliest Youth,
Had kept a Strict Regard for Truth,
Attempted to Believe Matilda:
The effort very nearly killed her,
And would have done so, had not She
Discovered this Infirmity.
For once, towards the Close of Day,
Matilda, growing tired of play,
And finding she was left alone,
Went tiptoe to the Telephone
And summoned the Immediate Aid
Of London's Noble Fire-Brigade.
Within an hour the Gallant Band
Were pouring in on every hand,
From Putney, Hackney Downs, and Bow
With Courage high and Hearts a-glow
They galloped, roaring through the Town,
"Matilda's House is Burning Down!"
Inspired by British Cheers and Loud
Proceeding from the Frenzied Crowd,
They ran their ladders through a score
Of windows on the Ball Room Floor;

And took Peculiar Pains to Souse
The Pictures up and down the House,
Until Matilda's Aunt succeeded
In showing them they were not needed;
And even then she had to pay
To get the Men to go away!

It happened that a few Weeks later
Her Aunt was off to the Theatre
To see that Interesting Play
The Second Mrs. Tanqueray.
She had refused to take her Niece
To hear this Entertaining Piece:
A Deprivation Just and Wise
To Punish her for Telling Lies.
That Night a Fire *did* break out—
You should have heard Matilda Shout!
You should have heard her Scream and Bawl,
And throw the window up and call
To People passing in the Street—
(The rapidly increasing Heat
Encouraging her to obtain
Their confidence)—but all in vain!
For every time She shouted "Fire!"
They only answered "Little Liar!"
And therefore when her Aunt returned,
Matilda, and the House, were Burned.

Eletelephony

Laura Richards

Once there was an elephant,
Who tried to use the telephant—
No! No! I mean an elephone
Who tried to use the telephone—
(Dear me! I am not certain quite
That even now I've got it right.)

Howe'er it was, he got his trunk
Entangled in the telephunk;
The more he tried to get it free,
The louder buzzed the telephee—
(I fear I'd better drop the song
Of elephop and telephong!)

Logical English

Anonymous

I said, "This horse, sir, will you shoe?"
  And soon the horse was shod.
I said, "This deed, sir, will you do?"
  And soon the deed was dod!

I said, "This stick, sir, will you break?"
  At once the stick he broke.
I said, "This coat, sir, will you make?"
  And soon the coat he moke!

Brush Up on Your English

Anonymous

I take it you already know
Of tough and bough and cough and dough
Others may stumble, but not you
On hiccough, thorough, laugh, and through.

And cork and work and card and ward
And font and front and word and sword
Well done! And now if you wish, perhaps
To learn of less familiar traps.

Beware of heard, a dreadful word
That looks like beard and sounds like bird.
And dead: It's said like bed and not like bead—
For goodness sakes don't call it deed.

Watch out for meat and great and threat,
They rhyme with suite and straight and debt.
A moth is not a moth in mothers,
Nor both in bother, broth in brother.

And here is not a match for there,
And dear and fear for bear and pear.
And then there's dose and rose and lose—
Just look them up—and goose and choose,

And do and go, then thwart and cart.
Come, come, I've hardly made a start!
A dreadful language? Man alive!
I'd mastered it when I was five.

Lines and Squares

A. A. Milne

Whenever I walk in a London street,
I'm ever so careful to watch my feet;
   And I keep in the squares,
   And the masses of bears,
Who wait at the corners all ready to eat
The sillies who tread on the lines of the street,
   Go back to their lairs,
   And I say to them, "Bears,
   Just look how I'm walking in all of the squares!"

And the little bears growl to each other, "He's mine,
As soon as he's silly and steps on a line."
And some of the bigger bears try to pretend
That they came round the corner to look for a friend;
And they try to pretend that nobody cares
Whether you walk on the lines or squares.
But only the sillies believe their talk;
It's ever so portant how you walk.
And it's ever so jolly to call out, "Bears,
Just watch me walking in all the squares!"

The Jumblies

Edward Lear

1

They went to sea in a sieve, they did;
   In a sieve they went to sea:
In spite of all their friends could say,
On a winter's morn, on a stormy day,
   In a sieve they went to sea.
And when the sieve turned round and round,
And every one cried, "You'll all be drowned!"
They called aloud, "Our sieve ain't big;
But we don't care a button, we don't care a fig:
   In a sieve we'll go to sea!"
     Far and few, far and few,
      Are the lands where the Jumblies live:
      Their heads are green, and their hands are blue;
       And they went to sea in a sieve.

2

They sailed away in a sieve, they did,
   In a sieve they sailed so fast,
With only a beautiful pea-green veil
Tied with a ribbon, by way of a sail,
   To a small tobacco-pipe mast
And every one said who saw them go,
"Oh! won't they be soon upset, you know?
For the sky is dark, and the voyage is long;

And, happen what may, it's extremely wrong
   In a sieve to sail so fast."
      Far and few, far and few,
         Are the lands where the Jumblies live:
       Their heads are green, and their hands are blue;
         And they went to sea in a sieve.

3

The water it soon came in, it did;
   The water it soon came in:
So, to keep them dry, they wrapped their feet
In a pinky paper all folded neat;
   And they fastened it down with a pin.
And they passed the night in a crockery-jar;
And each of them said, "How wise we are!
Though the sky be dark, and the voyage be long,
Yet we never can think we were rash or wrong,
   While round in our sieve we spin."
      Far and few, far and few,
         Are the lands where the Jumblies live:
       Their heads are green, and their hands are blue;
         And they went to sea in a sieve.

4

And all night long they sailed away;
   And when the sun went down,
They whistled and warbled a moony song
To the echoing sound of a coppery gong,
   In the shade of the mountains brown.

"O Timballoo! How happy we are
When we live in a sieve and a crockery-jar!
And all night long, in the moonlight pale,
We sail away with a pea-green sail
   In the shade of the mountains brown."
      Far and few, far and few,
         Are the lands where the Jumblies live:
         Their heads are green, and their hands are blue;
            And they went to sea in a sieve.

5

They sailed to the Western Sea, they did,—
   To a land all covered with trees:
And they bought an owl, and a useful cart,
And a pound of rice, and a cranberry-tart,
   And a hive of silvery bees;
And they bought a pig, and some green jackdaws,
And a lovely monkey with lollipop paws,
And forty bottles of ring-bo-ree,
   And no end of Stilton cheese.
      Far and few, far and few,
         Are the lands where the Jumblies live:
         Their heads are green, and their hands are blue;
            And they went to sea in a sieve.

6

And in twenty years they all came back,—
    In twenty years or more;
And every one said, "How tall they've grown!
For they've been to the Lakes, and the Torrible Zone,
    And the hills of the Chankly Bore."
And they drank their health, and gave them a feast
Of dumplings made of beautiful yeast;
And every one said, "If we only live,
We, too, will go to sea in a sieve,
    To the hills of the Chankly Bore."
      Far and few, far and few,
        Are the lands where the Jumblies live:
        Their heads are green, and their hands are blue;
        And they went to sea in a sieve.

The Pobble Who Has No Toes

Edward Lear

1

The Pobble who has no toes
   Had once as many as we;
When they said, "Some day you may lose them all";
   He replied, "Fish fiddle de-dee!"
And his Aunt Jobiska made him drink
Lavender water tinged with pink;
For she said, "The World in general knows
There's nothing so good for a Pobble's toes!"

2

The Pobble who has no toes,
   Swam across the Bristol Channel;
But before he set out he wrapped his nose
   In a piece of scarlet flannel.
For his Aunt Jobiska said, "No harm
Can come to his toes if his nose is warm;
And it's perfectly known that a Pobble's toes
Are safe—provided he minds his nose."

3

The Pobble swam fast and well,
   And when boats or ships came near him,
He tinkledy-binkledy-winkled a bell
   So that all the world could hear him.

And all the Sailors and Admirals cried,
When they saw him nearing the further side,—
"He has gone to fish, for his Aunt Jobiska's
Runcible Cat with crimson whiskers!"

4

But before he touched the shore,—
   The shore of the Bristol Channel,
A sea-green Porpoise carried away
   His wrapper of scarlet flannel.
And when he came to observe his feet,
Formerly garnished with toes so neat,
His face at once became forlorn
On perceiving that all his toes were gone!

5

And nobody ever knew,
   From that dark day to the present,
Whoso had taken the Pobble's toes,
   In a manner so far from pleasant.
Whether the shrimps or crawfish gray,
Or crafty Mermaids stole them away,
Nobody knew; and nobody knows
How the Pobble was robbed of his twice five toes!

6

The Pobble who has no toes
   Was placed in a friendly Bark,
And they rowed him back, and carried him up
   To his Aunt Jobiska's Park.

And she made him a feast, at his earnest wish,
Of eggs and buttercups fried with fish;
And she said, "It's a fact the whole world knows,
That Pobbles are happier without their toes."

The Owl and the Pussy-Cat

Edward Lear

1

The Owl and the Pussy-Cat went to sea
  In a beautiful pea-green boat:
They took some honey, and plenty of money
  Wrapped up in a five-pound note.
The Owl looked up to the stars above,
  And sang to a small guitar,
"O lovely Pussy, O Pussy, my love,
  What a beautiful Pussy you are,
      You are,
      You are!
  What a beautiful Pussy you are!"

2

Pussy said to the Owl, "You elegant fowl,
  How charmingly sweet you sing!
Oh! let us be married; too long we have tarried:
  But what shall we do for a ring?"
They sailed away, for a year and a day,
  To the land where the bong-tree grows;
And there in a wood a Piggy-wig stood,
  With a ring at the end of his nose,
      His nose,
      His nose,
  With a ring at the end of his nose.

3

"Dear Pig, are you willing to sell for one shilling
    Your ring?" Said the Piggy, "I will."
So they took it away, and were married next day
    By the Turkey who lives on the hill.
They dined on mince and slices of quince,
    Which they ate with a runcible spoon;
And hand in hand, on the edge of the sand,
    They danced by the light of the moon,
        The moon,
        The moon,
    They danced by the light of the moon.

The Purple Cow

Gelett Burgess

I never saw a Purple Cow,
I never hope to see one,
But I can tell you, anyhow,
I'd rather see than be one!

Table Manners

Gelett Burgess

The Goops they lick their fingers,
   And the Goops they lick their knives;
They spill their broth on the tablecloth—
   Oh, they lead disgusting lives!
The Goops they talk while eating,
   And loud and fast they chew;
And that is why I'm glad that I
   Am not a Goop—are you?

As I Was Walking up the Stair

Hughes Mearns

As I was walking up the stair
I met a man who wasn't there;
He wasn't there again today.
I wish, I wish he'd stay away.

Daddy Fell into the Pond

Alfred Noyes

Everyone grumbled. The sky was gray.
We had nothing to do and nothing to say.
We were nearing the end of a dismal day,
And there seemed to be nothing beyond,
   THEN
    Daddy fell into the pond!

And everyone's face grew merry and bright,
And Timothy danced for sheer delight.
"Give me the camera, quick, oh quick!
He's crawling out of the duckweed." *Click!*

Then the gardener suddenly slapped his knee,
And doubled up, shaking silently,
And the ducks all quacked as if they were daft
And it sounded as if the old drake laughed.

Oh, there wasn't a thing that didn't respond
   WHEN
    Daddy fell into the pond!

I Wandered Lonely as a Clod

The Editors of *MAD* Magazine

I wandered lonely as a clod
Just picking up old rags and bottles,
When onward on my way I plod,
I saw a host of axolotls;
Beside the lake, beneath the trees,
A sight to make a man's blood freeze.

Some had handles, some were plain;
They came in blue, red, pink, and green.
A few were orange in the main;
The damndest sight I've ever seen.
The females gave a sprightly glance;
The male ones all wore knee-length pants.

Now oft, when on the couch I lie,
The doctor asks me what I see.
They flash upon my inward eye
And make me laugh in fiendish glee.
I find my solace then in bottles,
And I forget them axolotls.

Acknowledgments

"The Adventures of Isabel" by Ogden Nash. Copyright © 1936 by Odgen Nash. Reprinted by permission of Curtis Brown, Ltd.

"April Rain Song" from *The Collected Poems of Langston Hughes* by Langston Hughes, edited by Arnold Rampersad with David Roessel, copyright © 1994 by the Estate of Langston Hughes. Used by permission of Alfred A. Knopf, a division of Random House, Inc.

"Counting Out Rhyme" copyright © 1928, 1955 by Edna St. Vincent Millay and Norma Millay Ellis. Reprinted by permission of Elizabeth Barnett, Literary Executor, The Millay Society.

"Daddy Fell into the Pond" by Alfred Noyes. © 1952. Reprinted by permission of The Society of Authors.

"Eletelephony" from *Tirra Lirra* by Laura Richards. Copyright © 1930, 1932 by Laura E. Richards; copyright © renewed 1960 by Hamilton Richards. By permission of Little, Brown and Company.

"Falling Up" by Shel Silverstein. Copyright © 1996. Evil Eye Music, Inc. Used by permission of HarperCollins Publishers.

"I Wandered Lonely as a Clod." © 1958 E.C. Publications, Inc. All Rights Reserved. Used with Permission.

"Lines and Squares" from *When We Were Very Young* by A. A. Milne, illustrations by E. H. Shepard, copyright © 1924 by E. P. Dutton, renewed 1952 by A. A. Milne. Used by permission of Dutton Children's Books, A Division of Penguin Young Readers Group, A Member of Penguin Group (USA) Inc., 345 Hudson Street, New York, NY 10014. All rights reserved.

Index to Titles and Authors